MASTER KEYS TO PREVENT
Road Rage

Develt Clay and Maria

Copyright © 2023 Develt Clay and Maria
All rights reserved
First Edition

NEWMAN SPRINGS PUBLISHING
320 Broad Street
Red Bank, NJ 07701

First originally published by Newman Springs Publishing 2023

ISBN 978-1-68498-039-0 (Paperback)
ISBN 978-1-68498-040-6 (Digital)

Printed in the United States of America

This book is dedicated to the ones who have lost their lives to the unproductive behavior of road rage. May the Lord bless your souls and correct the evil that is taking place behind the wheel of motor vehicles as drivers drive toward their destination. Protect them. Master key: do not fear.

This book was designed to assist every reader to form a strategy to prevent road rage. This format is a profitable read, and once again, it's my pleasure to assist mankind on how to prevent road rage while driving.

Please do enjoy your read!

Contents

About the Book vii
1 Practice at Staying Calm 1
2 Remind Yourself 6
3 Do Not Get Out of Your Vehicle 11
4 Do Not Pull Over 14

About the Book

Greetings. Welcome to *Master Keys to Prevent Road Rage*. Allow me this opportunity to introduce myself. My name is Develt Clay, and my coauthor is Maria. It's our honor and pleasure to present a host of master keys that could assist an individual to handle a great deal of road rage. These particular keys are a cornerstone for a person to stay strong under the pressure when confronted with the toxic energy of road rage. Here's a powerful master key to embrace.

These master keys could assist a driver to upgrade concerning the mindset as well as their emotions during uncomfortable moments when road rage is present. This is a must. There has to be a solid foundation concerning emotions when a driver is being cut off or called an unprofitable name from a "road-rager." What would you do in this situation? This is the million-dollar question.

Mind you, the reason why this book is essential is because a great deal of individuals have lost their lives to road rage. Step your game up on this matter if you need to because road rage is a toxic energy that releases tension between two drivers, and the result of this negative behavior is violence—and in some cases, death.

1

Practice at Staying Calm

In this particular chapter, we will be discussing a major cornerstone that could keep out the toxic energy that is operating on our streets with individuals who are operating motor vehicles.

Here's a power key to embrace: it is essential to learn how to stay strong and calm during the moment of road rage and its unproductive energy. This particular chapter is the four legs that hold this foundation together concerning preventing road rage.

An individual must learn how to remain calm under the negative energy and pressure of road rage. If an individual desires to upgrade in this area, they must encounter this process.

Here's the key: as humans, we are emotional individuals. We are people of habits, and without a balance concerning emotions, it would be easy to act up on impulse, meaning to act out without thinking. As a result of this unproductive behavior, in most cases, this would end with negative consequences, and for some, it was death.

Here's a powerful statement that I enjoy embracing: never allow anyone to see you sweat, meaning don't let anyone see you lose your cool or find it as an easy task to punch your buttons to get you angry.

Think about what you are thinking about

Power key: this first segment that I would like to present to you is essential. Please do dissect this statement. Think about what you are thinking about when confronted with road rage. Here's why I say that: whenever you are encountered with road rage while driving, remember to think about what you are thinking about, meaning to make sure that you aren't feeding negative thoughts that road rage feeds on. Think about what would/could happen if you feed into road rage. Don't allow the toxic energy of road rage to take hold of you as you drive to your destination.

Remember, readers, there are consequences for your actions if you would allow your emotions to do something that may be out of your character within a moment of road rage.

Power key: keep in mind as you drive your vehicle that a great deal of individuals are driving vehicles like they are out-of-control bullets. They don't care about the well-being of mankind, not even themselves. So why would road rage care about you? It's essential to think on a productive level when driving as well as to think and drive for others.

Utilize these tools

Here's something to reflect on: a great deal of individuals who are driving on society's roads today are heartless, and please do be mindful that a host of them are seeking out individuals to inflict pain on. Most of these people, in some cases, don't have a family to provide for nor a profession that they may look forward to. Here's my master key that I am placing on the table before you.

Don't allow anyone to cause you to step outside of your character due to someone that may cut you off in traffic or call you an unproductive name that would cause you to stop your vehicle. Always keep it moving. Never stop!

You have to remember that most individuals who are controlled by road rage don't care about anything or anyone, not even you. They are willing to put their life on the line because someone isn't going fast enough or someone looked at them due to their unproductive behavior.

MASTER KEYS TO PREVENT ROAD RAGE

Don't lose your cool

Power key: don't allow anyone to make you lose your cool and argue. Never allow anyone to see you sweat. Please do embrace this rare master key because it could save an individual a great deal of confusion and toxic energy in the near future.

This reminds me of how my life in the past was so immature when road rage is concerned. I had to learn how to control my emotions when it comes to the behavior of road-ragers.

I had to step my game up in this area, and it required me to be honest with myself to address this matter because it was really easy for me to challenge another driver when I was innocent in the matter.

The reality of this matter is that I acted on my emotions and not the strategy that you and I are forming through this book. I was blessed to make it through some encounters concerning road rage because today, an individual would shoot through their window in a heartbeat.

Keep it simple

Keep it simple and stay calm by utilizing this particular format as a strategy to overcome the toxic energy that comes from road rage.

A few days ago, I was waiting for a family member to come out of a local store. I was waiting in my vehicle. A car had run out of gas. As a result, a number of vehicles were lined up, blowing their horns at the lady who ran out of gas. A few drivers went around her, and as they were driving away, one of them yelled from the car window, "You are a (name that I don't want to say)!"

I was saddened to see how our streets have become a war zone mixed with hate and anger.

I walked over to the line of cars that were blowing their horns and asked her, "Do you want me to assist you to push your car out from traffic?" The line of cars watched me push the car to the side as the other cars continued to drive through the intersection.

Don't feed toxic energy

Here's my point: no one asked her if she needed help. Instead, they degraded her as if she was doing something wrong because she ran out of gasoline. I believe that every driver could relate to that to some degree.

However, I don't believe that the anger wasn't rising from the lack of gasoline but the toxic energy from road rage.

As the individuals drove by us, the look in their eyes exposed the secrets of their hearts concerning how they felt about mankind.

It placed joy in my heart to assist her to regain mobility and to continue to her destination. Toxic energy is a negative force that seeks individuals out to connect to their emotions.

The reality is that a large number of individuals who act out in negative behavior don't realize that they are controlled by this unproductive energy. Here are a few signs to look for when this energy is present: angry for no reason, not sensitive to mankind, or ready to become violent and hurt or kill someone for a small matter without the thought of a discussion.

Understand how negative energy works

Think about what you are thinking about if you are confronted with road rage, meaning to stop yourself from becoming angry. Learn to take one for the team, your husband or wife, or your family. Remember what truly matters at the moment.

It's the road rager who is trying to destroy your life and trying to remove you from the equation of your loved ones who need you and are waiting for you to return home. Don't allow anyone to rob you of that.

It's essential to stay calm when confronted with road rage. It doesn't make you out to be a weak individual but a smart one who is a thinker and not a person that moves on impulse, meaning to act without thinking.

MASTER KEYS TO PREVENT ROAD RAGE

This is the first segment of our process that is highlighted so that you could be conscious of your thoughts and so that you could defuse the toxic energy that you may be confronted with.

Once again, reader, this process that we are discussing is a major cornerstone that this material is based on.

I highly recommend that you take your time and read this material at a slow pace. Don't rush through it just to complete reading the book. Here's why: because this format of information holds a host of master keys that could assist you in saving your life.

2

Remind Yourself

In this particular chapter, we are going to discuss a powerful strategy that is essential when it comes to a mental note when you need to be reminded. Remind yourself if you need to have your own back. As a matter of fact, I utilize this strategy in many different realms of life. I learned to be able to encourage myself if I need to.

When caught off guard with an individual who is trying to inflict you with toxic energy, a person must be prepared to think their way through an unproductive encounter.

However, the sad aspect of this narrative is that a great number of individuals fail this test because they are acting on emotions opposed to preparation and strategy.

If you ever saw two individuals experiencing a moment of road rage, you can't help but notice the negative energy that would be operating out-of-control anger. Over what? What if one of the individuals made a mistake and wanted to apologize, but they were verbally abused before they opened their mouth. The sad aspect of this matter is that some may have died by the hands of a road-rager before they could say, "I apologize."

Think before you react

Power key: think before you react because today, we have a host of individuals driving around with guns, and in some cases, they may be looking for someone to try it on. Sick but true. It's essential to think before you react.

Here's the reality: you would never know who may drive next to you at a stoplight or may try to run into your vehicle so that you could stop your car. Being prepared is my sole mission for my readers. Please do embrace these master keys.

Always be aware when toxic energy presents itself to you. Do not get emotional, meaning do not fall apart and lose control and allow the toxic energy to take you hostage.

Stay calm and stick to the plan of preparation, and you would have a higher chance to make it home to your family. Remind yourself the times are evil, and you must be prepared for them.

The truth is that a great deal of individuals find it uncomfortable discussing topics such as these. But for me, it's a reality. However, unfortunately, everyone would face road rage to some degree.

It's a reality in our streets.

Let's face it! It's a reality that violence and road rage is prevalent in our streets. Is it going to go away? Sad to say, but no! However, that doesn't mean that an individual shouldn't prepare themselves to the best of their ability so that a negative person controlled by road rage won't affect their life.

Here's my master key: preparation for road rage is a shell of protection which is a format of being a thinker, someone who thinks outside of the box, someone who could outthink a situation. Emotions can't do it. Only a productive strategy can. Delete all negative thoughts when confronted with road rage.

This particular book that you are now holding is a wise investment that I believe every individual that operates a motor vehicle should read. Why? Because everyone who would drive an automobile would encounter road rage to some degree, and we can't be in denial of this unprofitable matter.

Here's the process

Master key: after reading this material, I encourage you to start the process of preparation by taking time out to delete negative thoughts when they rise within your mindset. Here's why this homework is essential. Please do grant me the opportunity to give you a reason for the lesson.

Preparation means to prepare to execute. We don't waste time for road rage to come to us. We prepare to execute it when it presents itself. Negative thoughts are connected to road rage.

Here's the requirement for road rage. In order for road rage to manifest itself, it requires two or more angry individuals to come together. Here's the process when two or more angry individuals come together in the motion of anger; the force of that energy exacerbates the matter to another whole level which in most cases always ends with a degree of violence.

Individuals' thoughts are the root problem of road rage, not the act per se, because if the mindset of road-ragers was productive, then the negative behavior would be deleted. Also, this process of deleting negative thoughts has great benefits, not just as you drive, but this could apply in every realm of life.

Thoughts have power

Deleting toxic thoughts continues to anger people. As you may know, thoughts control them as well. Thoughts control productive individuals' behaviors also. It's the force behind the thoughts.

For example, toxic energy rises from a negative force that keeps a person going into a downward slope opposed to a productive vibe that motivates individuals to reach for the stars in life. In most cases, only a productive mindset would continue to read a book such as this one that you now hold.

I recommend a powerful tool to utilize to keep your mindset clear to practice at deleting negative thoughts when they enter your mind. In most cases, you may have to delete them until they begin to fade away from your mind.

Remember, this process doesn't work on it's own. You can't do it one time and expect the toxic thought to leave. You have to work this process until it works for you.

MASTER KEYS TO PREVENT ROAD RAGE

If you decide to work this format, you will thank me later for this process that you are reading at this moment concerning this rare material.

Power note: preparation is the format of being a thinker. It is wisdom that grants you the understanding to prepare yourself to execute your goals.

Control your thinking

Here's a master key to embrace: your thoughts control your behavior, each event that we face on a daily basis; our thought pattern would determine the outcome, whether it would be productive or nonproductive. There are consequences for what we think.

Preparation is essential because road rage would catch an individual off guard. If a person's emotions are not in check to some degree, an individual would have to be able to check their emotions. If not, as you may already know, the impact of road rage would get the best of them.

I recommend you begin practicing this format as soon as possible. Do not take road rage lightly. Learn to control your thinking.

I can recall a particular time a guy was riding my bumper. He was so close to me that if I had hit the brakes, he would have hit me.

What do you do in that kind of situation? Have you ever been there? What did you say to yourself as this unproductive encounter was in motion?

For me, I was angry, and I felt the tension of road rage all over me. I had to learn how to defuse the power of it by outthinking it.

Don't be a hearer but a doer

Master key: the thought pattern is a weapon. It could give an individual an increase or a decrease. That decision would be up to the individual. We all must decide to grow or upgrade in particular areas in our lives. No one can change it for us. We have to upgrade for ourselves.

Unfortunately, concerning the matter of upgrading, a host of individuals prefer to remain the same because upgrading could be uncomfortable. It is not meant to be comfortable.

Master note: never stop growing mentally. Always keep the growing process active, and you will be amazed at yourself concerning your growth increase.

Don't just listen to this format but be a doer of it. Once again, it's my pleasure to present this material, and may you become much wiser in this area concerning road rage.

Don't allow road rage to continue to have power over you. Break all ties to it today and be free from its bondage.

3

Do Not Get Out of Your Vehicle

In this particular chapter, we will be discussing a major link in this process that is called your defense system, meaning do not get out of your vehicle when confronted with road rage.

This reminds me of a road rage experience I viewed some months ago. I was sitting in my vehicle at a red light. As I looked into my mirror, I saw two vehicles coming behind me at a high speed. I moved over to let them through.

One of the vehicles was driving bumper-to-bumper with the other vehicle as the driver in the front was yelling at the driver behind them. It was like a motion movie in action. The two individuals exited from their vehicles, filled with road rage. The tension was so intense that I felt it in my vehicle.

The two individuals attacked one another as if they were fighting for their lives. I didn't believe what I was seeing! Pure uncut road rage in motion.

Road rage could turn bad at any given time. Don't take it lightly. Be prepared and positioned to drive away safe when confronted with a road rage encounter.

Stick to the plan

No matter what happens, do not get out of your vehicle during a road rage experience. Do not stop your vehicle unless it is an emergency stop, meaning that you don't have a choice. Stick to the plan.

Sticking to the plan is a segment of the preparation process. I must add as well that this principle applies to life encounters in general.

Here's a major cornerstone that is profitable concerning decision-making. A strategy would give an individual a 95 percent chance of being successful at whatever the task may be at hand. This is a powerful master key to embrace in life.

Emotions without a balance could be a liability as opposed to an asset. Why do I say that? Because unbalanced emotions move without thinking. It is like an out-of-control vehicle coming at you.

It's okay to grow

Power note: I highlight the word *preparation/strategy* because this foundation is the ground for success concerning road rage as well.

It's okay to grow mentally, and once again, never stop upgrading your character because it would release a great return when you may really need it, such as preparing yourself to execute road rage.

You are upgrading yourself at this very moment by viewing information on this particular topic concerning road rage.

Allow me this opportunity to give you a high five! It's a great encounter to know that you are still growing mentally. I am placing this format before you for a reason. To cause some to think again and to add knowledge. How valuable the word *preparation* is.

The reason I stated to think again is because the technology we have today has caused a great number of individuals to depend on their computers rather than on their minds.

MASTER KEYS TO PREVENT ROAD RAGE

Let's think again

Practice at being calm when you are dealing with uncomfortable moments in life. This would be a great starting point to prepare to position yourself to remain calm under pressure.

Here's the power key: whenever we find ourselves in the midst of a degree of pressure, it would show an individual what they are truly made of. Who are you under pressure?

Who are you when someone cuts you off in traffic? Who are you when someone is riding your bumper? Who are you under road rage pressure?

The good aspect about that question is that we are dealing with a solution to find a great deal of closure to this unprofitable matter called road rage.

It's essential to be mindful that when we operate a motor vehicle, it is imperative to think for other drivers, meaning to get out of the way if you need to.

Let's think again. We have to learn how to outthink road rage with a strategy and not emotions.

4

Do Not Pull Over

In this chapter, we are going to discuss a technique that drivers must embrace concerning the format of road rage. It is essential when an individual is confronted with the toxic energy of road rage.

When confronted with road rage, do not stop your vehicle or pull over for no reason unless you are having car trouble.

Power key: be aware of your surroundings. Once again, you have to learn to outthink the negative energy of road rage.

Personally, I learned to pull over and allow a road-rager to pass. It's simple to defuse the negative force that is trying to take you hostage as you utilize this technique by letting the road-rager pass. In most cases, they would speed by you as if they are on diplomatic business.

The reality of this process is that the negative energy of road rage is controlling that individual who is driving the vehicle. They are in such a hurry that they don't have any concern for the well-being of others, and for some road-ragers, not even for themselves.

Be wise

Keep your motor vehicle in motion when road rage is present. It would be wise as well not to give a road-rager full eye contact but a glance and keep it moving.

MASTER KEYS TO PREVENT ROAD RAGE

Here's the key: if a road-rager tries to force you to go faster to their pace or rides your bumper at a close level, pull your vehicle over and allow them to pass. Be wise when dealing with an individual who is trying to make you speed up or lose your cool behind the wheel.

Once again, keep your vehicle moving because road rage could only act on another individual's emotions. Without this process taking place, road rage wouldn't have any power. It takes two individuals to agree.

It takes two individuals to agree on a task. The negative force cannot operate until two people are taken hostage by the evil force of road rage.

Road rage seeks out individuals' emotions to link to. It cannot operate when a person defuses its power while driving in a motor vehicle. Road rage tests individuals' emotions. Don't allow it to get you.

Do not listen to negative voices

Here's a master key to embrace that could release a grand return if you are wise enough to receive it. Stop listening to negative voices that you may encounter when it comes to being confronted with road rage. Stay focused and stay calm. A road-rager's behavior is a form of toxic energy that is waiting to conflict it on the next driver.

Power note: don't allow any road-rager to be able to punch your buttons and cause you to become angry and curse with profanity. This is what you could consider to be a heated moment. Be prepared to maintain a productive mindset when road rage presents itself.

However, this book is designed to assist an individual to learn how to prevent road rage and to create a handle on this unprofitable matter. This format that you are viewing is a process. Practicing these principles doesn't work overnight. It's a process. Here's the master key to this book. As you begin to work this format, then this format will work for you.

Once again, each day, start the process of deleting negative thoughts by saying, "Today, I'm going to think of productive thoughts." And when a negative thought rises, tell yourself, "No negative thoughts today." This is the first process of gaining some degree of control over your mindset.

In closing, it's time for a change

Power key: think positive when it comes to this book, and it will work for you concerning dealing with road rage. It's my pleasure and honor to present this material to you.

This process also applies to encountering all negative situations. These are power keys to help an individual to become stronger when it comes to the behavior of others.

I leave you with a rare jewel of advice: a positive mindset is always a great ground to receive a handsome return on your time.

This is a Royalty Foundation presentation. We hope that this information has been a stepping-stone to assist you to take your game to another level.

Once again, it's been our pleasure.

Develt Clay and Maria

About the Author

Hello, readers, once again, my name is Develt Clay, and my coauthor is Maria. It's our honor to present this material to you today. It's our pleasure. We felt a strong need to release this lifeline to all drivers.

This material is to assist all automobile drivers to maintain a productive mindset during unproductive moments while encountering road rage that all drivers would face to some degree.

Our mission as authors is to educate drivers to think smart and to stay calm while confronted with toxic energy while driving. A peaceful mindset is essential because it could help an individual to save their life as well as someone else's.

This particular book isn't about the authors; it is based on assisting a driver to defuse negative energy that is operating in our streets in society. This book is a wise choice.

Think about the information that is placed on the table before you today. These are a host of master keys that could assist you to create a strategy to defuse the negative energy of road rage. Please do enjoy your read.

www.ingramcontent.com/pod-product-compliance
Lightning Source LLC
Chambersburg PA
CBHW031659040426
42453CB00006B/350